AMOXICILLIN

A Comprehensive Guide to Treating Pneumonia, Respiratory Infections, UTIs, Otitis Media, Dental Infections, and More Using Antibiotics

Jacob Ryan

Copyright © 2024 Jacob Ryan

All rights reserved. No part of this publication may be reproduced, distributed, or transmitted in any form of by any means, including photocopying, recording or other electronic or mechanical methods, without the prior written permission of the publisher, except in the case of brief quotations embodied in critical reviews and certain other noncommercial uses permitted by copyright law.

Legal Disclaimer

The information provided in this book, "AMOXICILLIN - A Comprehensive Guide to Treating Pneumonia, Respiratory Infections, UTIs, Otitis Media, Dental Infections, and More Using Antibiotics", is for general informational and educational purposes only. The author, Jacob Ryan, is not a licensed medical professional, and the content should not be considered a substitute for professional medical advice, diagnosis, or treatment.

Readers are encouraged to consult with their healthcare provider or a qualified medical professional before engaging in any treatment, especially if they have pre-existing health conditions or concerns.

Title | Amoxicillin
Author | Jacob Ryan

ISBN | 979-12-22777-33-7

© 2024. All rights reserved by the Author
This work is published directly by the Author via the Youcanprint self-publishing platform and the Author holds all rights thereto exclusively. No part of this book may therefore be reproduced without the prior consent of the Author.

Youcanprint
Via Marco Biagi 6, 73100 Lecce
www.youcanprint.it
info@youcanprint.it
Made by human

Table of Contents

Chapter 1: Understanding Amoxicillin _____ 7
  What is Amoxicillin? _____ 7
    Chemical Structure _____ 10
  Physical Properties of Amoxicillin _____ 11
  Melting Point _____ 11

Chapter 2: Conditions Treated by Amoxicillin _____ 13
  When is Amoxicillin Prescribed? _____ 13
    Respiratory Tract Infections (RTIs) _____ 14
    Common Cold _____ 15
    Influenza _____ 15
    Rhinosinusitis _____ 16
    Otitis Media (Middle Ear Infection) _____ 17
    Tonsillitis and Pharyngitis _____ 17

Chapter 3: Warnings and Precautions: What You Need to Know Before Taking Amoxicillin _____ 19
  What to Know before Taking Amoxicillin _____ 19
    Important Safety Information _____ 19
    Precautions and Warnings _____ 20
    Testing and Interactions _____ 21
    Interactions with Other Medications _____ 21
    Additional Considerations Before Using Amoxicillin _____ 22
    Drug-Drug Interactions _____ 23
    Other Interactions _____ 24

Chapter 4: How Amoxicillin Works _____ 27
  Mechanism of Action _____ 27

Absorption and Bioavailability	28
Distribution in the Body	28
Excretion and Metabolism	29
Mechanisms of Bacterial Resistance	29
Susceptibility Interpretive Criteria for Amoxicillin	30
Quality Control in Susceptibility Testing	31
Chapter 5: Pharmacological Interactions Between Amoxicillin and Other Drugs	**33**
Understanding Drug-Drug Interactions	33
Common Drug Interactions with Amoxicillin	34
Chapter 6: Dosage and Method of Application	**37**
General Guidelines for Taking Amoxicillin	37
Dosage Guidelines	38
Dosage for Specific Conditions	40
If You Miss a Dose	42
Chapter 7: Side Effects	**43**
Common Side Effects of Amoxicillin	43
Serious Side Effects of Amoxicillin	44
Managing Side Effects	45
Chapter 8: Pregnancy and Breastfeeding	**47**
Amoxicillin During Pregnancy	47
Other Safe Antibiotics During Pregnancy	48
Common Side Effects During Pregnancy	48
Serious Side Effects to Watch For	49
Potential Risks and Benefits	49
Pregnancy and Bacterial Infections	50
Breastfeeding While Using Amoxicillin	51
BONUS CHAPTER: FREQUENTLY ASKED QUESTIONS	**53**

Chapter 1: Understanding Amoxicillin

What is Amoxicillin?

Amoxicillin is a commonly prescribed antibiotic that belongs to the penicillin family. It is effective for treating a range of bacterial infections (but not viral infections) in various parts of the body, including:

- Respiratory system infections like sinus and chest infections
- Urinary tract infections (UTIs)
- Middle ear infections (otitis media)
- Dental infections

Doctors may prescribe amoxicillin if there is a high risk of bacterial infection. It works by killing the bacteria responsible for these infections, specifically by disrupting their cell walls, which leads to their elimination.

Did You Know?

Amoxicillin is also used to treat infections caused by Helicobacter pylori, a bacterium linked to stomach ulcers. Patients with stomach ulcers often take amoxicillin in combination with other medications to improve treatment effectiveness.

Type of Medicine:

Penicillin antibiotic.

Used For:

Bacterial infections in adults and children.

Available Forms:

Amoxicillin comes in several forms, including capsules, oral liquid, dissolvable tablets, sachets of powder, and injections.

A Brief History of Amoxicillin

Amoxicillin was developed in 1972 by scientists at Beecham Research Laboratories. Researchers had been looking for penicillin-based antibiotics that could treat a broader range of infections. Ampicillin was an earlier breakthrough that allowed doctors to treat both gram-positive and gram-negative bacterial infections, which are classified based on the structure of their cell walls.

Building on ampicillin, researchers developed amoxicillin, which has a slightly longer half-life (duration in the body) and a unique structural feature—a hydroxyl (OH) group on its benzene ring. This adjustment gives amoxicillin slightly better solubility in lipids, potentially allowing it to act faster in eliminating bacteria.

How Amoxicillin Works

Amoxicillin targets bacterial cell walls, a crucial structure for bacteria's survival. It prevents the formation of peptidoglycan chains, the main building blocks of cell walls. This disruption stops the bacteria from growing and eventually leads to their death.

Chemical Structure

Amoxicillin's chemical structure includes a penicillin backbone with modifications that enhance its effectiveness. It has a benzene ring with an added hydroxyl (OH) group, distinguishing it from other antibiotics in the penicillin family.

Physical Properties of Amoxicillin

- **Form**: Amoxicillin typically exists as amoxicillin trihydrate, with a unique crystal structure that influences its stability.
- **Crystal Structure**: When analyzed using X-ray diffraction, amoxicillin crystals were found to have a structure known as orthorhombic, with specific atoms arranged in a tight structure. This arrangement, along with hydrogen bonding, gives amoxicillin stability and helps it retain its crystalline form.
- **Stability and Crystallinity**: Amoxicillin trihydrate maintains some crystalline properties even after dehydration. In contrast, when ampicillin (another antibiotic in the penicillin family) is dehydrated, it loses its structure and becomes amorphous (lacking a clear form). This difference is due to the hydroxyl (OH) group in amoxicillin, which makes it structurally more stable than ampicillin.

Melting Point

Melting Point: 194°C.

Amoxicillin has been an essential antibiotic since its development, used to treat a variety of infections effectively and with relatively few side effects. Its specific chemical structure provides stability and enables it to act quickly against harmful bacteria, making it one of the most widely used antibiotics in the world.

Chapter 2: Conditions Treated by Amoxicillin

When is Amoxicillin Prescribed?

Amoxicillin is widely prescribed for bacterial infections affecting various parts of the body, including the respiratory system, urinary tract, and skin. As a penicillin-like antibiotic, it works by inhibiting bacterial growth, helping the immune system to clear the infection. However, it is ineffective against viral infections, like the common cold.

Note: Using antibiotics when unnecessary can contribute to antibiotic resistance. Always consult with a healthcare provider before starting any antibiotic treatment.

Common Conditions Treated with Amoxicillin:

- Respiratory Tract Infections (such as bronchitis and sinusitis)
- Ear, Nose, and Throat (ENT) Infections
- Urinary Tract Infections (UTIs)
- Skin Infections
- Helicobacter pylori infection (in combination with other medications for treating stomach ulcers)
- Lyme Disease (infections from tick bites)
- Anthrax prevention (when exposure is suspected)

Respiratory Tract Infections (RTIs)

Respiratory infections are among the most common reasons for doctor visits, particularly upper respiratory infections (URIs) like sinus infections and bronchitis. Antibiotics like amoxicillin can be necessary for bacterial respiratory infections but are often overprescribed, especially for viral illnesses like the common cold.

Examples of RTIs Treated with Amoxicillin:

- **Bronchitis**: Infection in the bronchial tubes that may require antibiotics if bacterial.
- **Rhinosinusitis**: Inflammation of the sinuses, which can be bacterial if symptoms persist beyond 10 days or worsen after initial improvement.

Common Cold

The common cold causes symptoms like a runny nose, sore throat, cough, and nasal congestion—all typically due to viral infections. Antibiotics, including amoxicillin, do not alleviate these viral symptoms. Studies show that antibiotics have little impact on URIs that are not caused by bacteria.

> *Tip: For viral infections, supportive care—like hydration, rest, and symptom management—is often the most effective approach.*

Influenza

Influenza, caused by the influenza virus, primarily affects the upper respiratory tract. While antiviral medications can reduce the duration of symptoms if started early, antibiotics like amoxicillin should only be considered if there is a secondary bacterial infection. In patients with severe symptoms or risk factors, such as the elderly or individuals with chronic conditions, medical consultation is crucial to determine if antibiotics are necessary.

Rhinosinusitis

Rhinosinusitis is an inflammation of the nasal passages and sinuses, often with symptoms such as purulent nasal discharge, facial pain, and reduced smell. Rhinosinusitis can be:

- **Acute** (lasting less than 4 weeks)
- **Subacute** (lasting 4-12 weeks)
- **Chronic** (persisting over 12 weeks)

Bacterial Rhinosinusitis is suspected if symptoms persist beyond 10 days or worsen after initial improvement. Mild cases can often resolve on their own, but antibiotics like amoxicillin may be prescribed for persistent or severe cases.

Table Suggestion: A table outlining symptoms that differentiate bacterial vs. viral rhinosinusitis could clarify when antibiotics are appropriate.

Otitis Media (Middle Ear Infection)

Otitis media is an infection of the middle ear, commonly affecting children. Bacteria such as Haemophilus influenzae, Streptococcus pneumoniae, and Moraxella catarrhalis are common culprits. In mild cases, especially in children older than six months, doctors may recommend "watchful waiting" to see if symptoms resolve before prescribing antibiotics.

Key Points for Treating Otitis Media:

- Children under two years with bilateral infections or severe symptoms may benefit from immediate antibiotic treatment.
- First-line therapy is often amoxicillin at a dose of 80-90 mg/kg per day, divided into two doses.
- If there's no response within 48-72 hours, another antibiotic may be needed.

Tonsillitis and Pharyngitis

Pharyngitis (sore throat) is mostly viral, but in cases caused by Group A Streptococcus (GAS), antibiotics like amoxicillin can help prevent complications like rheumatic fever.

Testing for Streptococcal Infection (GAS):

- Rapid Antigen Detection Test (RADT) can confirm bacterial pharyngitis, guiding the need for antibiotics.
- Only patients with a high likelihood of bacterial infection or confirmed test results should receive antibiotics to avoid unnecessary medication.

Amoxicillin is a powerful antibiotic for various bacterial infections. However, it should only be used for confirmed or strongly suspected bacterial infections to prevent resistance. Consulting a healthcare provider for the correct diagnosis is essential for effective treatment and avoiding unnecessary antibiotic use.

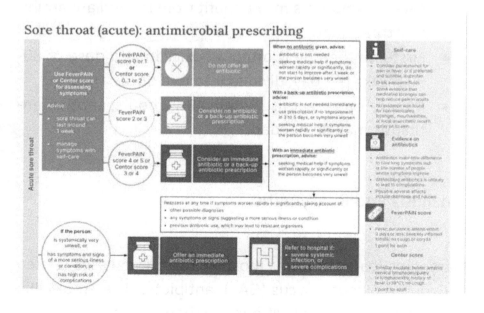

Chapter 3: Warnings and Precautions: What You Need to Know Before Taking Amoxicillin

What to Know before Taking Amoxicillin

Before starting amoxicillin, it's essential to understand possible side effects, precautions, and any interactions with other medications or health conditions. This chapter will guide you on safely using amoxicillin and recognizing signs that may require medical attention.

Important Safety Information

- **Consult your doctor** if symptoms do not improve or worsen after a few days.
- **Allergic Reactions**: Amoxicillin can cause a life-threatening allergic reaction called anaphylaxis. Seek emergency care if you experience symptoms like skin rash,

itchiness, difficulty breathing, or swelling in the face, hands, or mouth.
- **Diarrhea**: Amoxicillin may lead to severe diarrhea, which can occur even two months after stopping the medication. Avoid over-the-counter diarrhea treatments without consulting your doctor, as they may worsen symptoms.
- **Medical Tests**: Amoxicillin can influence some blood and urine tests, so inform your doctor if you are taking it before any lab tests.
- **Tooth Discoloration**: Some children may experience temporary tooth discoloration. Regular brushing and dental check-ups can help prevent this.
- **Birth Control Interaction**: Amoxicillin may reduce the effectiveness of birth control pills. Consider additional contraception methods, like condoms or diaphragms, to prevent pregnancy while on this medication.

If you're using hormonal birth control, consult your doctor about the best additional method to use while taking amoxicillin.

Precautions and Warnings

It's recommended to consult your doctor before taking amoxicillin if you:

- Have glandular fever (fever, sore throat, swollen glands, and fatigue)
- Have kidney problems
- Urinate infrequently.

Testing and Interactions

<u>Blood and Urine Tests:</u>

Amoxicillin can affect certain medical tests. Inform your healthcare provider if you are undergoing:

- Urine glucose tests (for diabetes)
- Blood liver function tests
- Oestriol tests (used during pregnancy to monitor baby's development).

Interactions with Other Medications

Tell your doctor or pharmacist if you are taking, recently took, or plan to take any other medications or supplements. Combining amoxicillin with certain medications may increase the risk of adverse effects or decrease effectiveness.

<u>Common Interactions:</u>

- **Allopurinol** (for gout) may increase the chance of skin reactions when combined with amoxicillin.
- **Warfarin** (anticoagulant) may require additional blood tests to monitor clotting.
- **Cancer medications** may increase the risk of side effects when taken with amoxicillin.

Here a table of common drug interactions with amoxicillin makes it easy for you to check specific medications:

- Chlortetracycline
- Cholera Vaccine, Live
- Demeclocycline
- Desogestrel
- Dienogest
- Doxycycline
- Drospirenone
- Eravacycline
- Estradiol
- Ethinyl Estradiol
- Ethynodiol
- Gestodene
- Levonorgestrel
- Lymecycline
- Meclocycline
- Mestranol
- Methacycline
- Methotrexate
- Minocycline
- Mycophenolate Mofetil
- Nomegestrol
- Norethindrone
- Norgestimate
- Norgestrel
- Omadacycline
- Oxytetracycline
- Rolitetracycline
- Sarecycline
- Sulfasalazine
- Tetracycline
- Tigecycline
- Venlafaxine
- Warfarin

Additional Considerations Before Using Amoxicillin

Allergies:

If you've experienced an adverse reaction to any medication, including penicillin, tell your doctor. People allergic to penicillins or cephalosporins (e.g., cefaclor, cephalexin) should avoid amoxicillin.

For Pediatric Use:

Amoxicillin is generally safe for children. However, infants younger than 12 weeks may require lower doses due to developing kidney function.

For Geriatric Patients:

While amoxicillin is effective in older adults, kidney function should be monitored closely to avoid potential side effects from slower drug elimination.

For Breastfeeding Mothers:

The safety of amoxicillin during breastfeeding is not fully established. Talk with your doctor to weigh the benefits and risks.

Drug-Drug Interactions

Sometimes, despite potential interactions, two drugs may be used together if your doctor adjusts the dosage or monitors your health. Inform your doctor if you're using any of the following medications, as they may interact with amoxicillin:

- **Acenocoumarol** (blood thinner)
- **Khat** (a herbal stimulant)
- **Probenecid** (used for gout).

Always keep an updated list of your medications to share with your healthcare provider. This helps identify potential interactions quickly.

Other Interactions

Certain medications should not be taken close to meals, while others interact with alcohol or tobacco. Check with your doctor or pharmacist to learn about any restrictions related to foods, beverages, or smoking when using amoxicillin.

Health Conditions to Consider:

If you have any of the following conditions, inform your doctor, as they may affect your use of amoxicillin:

- **Allergy** to Penicillins or Cephalosporins: If you are allergic to penicillin or cephalosporin antibiotics, discuss alternatives with your doctor.
- **Severe Kidney Disease**: Amoxicillin should be used with caution, as kidney impairment may increase its effects.
- **Phenylketonuria (PKU)**: Amoxicillin chewable tablets contain phenylalanine, which may be harmful to individuals with PKU.

If you have a condition that affects your body's ability to eliminate drugs, your doctor may adjust your amoxicillin dosage to ensure safe use.

Symptoms and Action Recommended:

- Skin rash, itchiness, swelling of face/hands/mouth?
  Seek emergency medical attention (possible allergic reaction).
- Shortness of breath or difficulty breathing?
  Seek emergency medical attention (possible allergic reaction)
- Diarrhea (severe or lasting over a week)?
  Consult doctor before using anti-diarrheal medications
- Persistent or worsening infection symptoms?

Consult doctor before using anti-diarrheal medications
- Unusual tooth discoloration in children?
Regular brushing or dental visits can help prevent staining
- Reduced effectiveness of birth control?
Use additional contraception methods; consult doctor if unsure.

Taking amoxicillin safely requires understanding potential side effects, interactions, and the importance of consulting a healthcare provider if symptoms persist. Knowing when to seek medical advice can help prevent complications and ensure effective treatment.

Chapter 4: How Amoxicillin Works

Amoxicillin is a **beta-lactam antibiotic**, a class known for its ability to kill bacteria by disrupting their cell walls. This chapter explores how amoxicillin interacts with bacterial cells, how it is absorbed and distributed in the body, and how resistance to it can develop.

Mechanism of Action

Amoxicillin kills bacteria by targeting specific proteins within the bacteria's cell wall. When these proteins are disrupted, the bacterial cell wall becomes unstable, leading to cell dissolution and death. This bactericidal (bacteria-killing) effect is effective only on bacteria actively growing or dividing.

> *Amoxicillin is ineffective against viruses, which lack cell walls. Using it for viral infections, like colds or the flu, will not help and can contribute to antibiotic resistance.*

Absorption and Bioavailability

When taken orally, amoxicillin is stable in stomach acid, allowing it to be easily absorbed into the bloodstream. The body's peak blood levels of amoxicillin occur within 1 to 2 hours after taking a dose, reaching typical concentrations of:

- **3.5 to 5.0 mcg/mL** for a 250 mg dose
- **5.5 to 7.5 mcg/mL** for a 500 mg dose

Food has minimal impact on amoxicillin absorption, making it a convenient option for patients who need flexibility with dosing times.

Distribution in the Body

Amoxicillin diffuses quickly throughout most tissues and body fluids, although it does not typically reach the brain and spinal fluid unless the meninges (protective coverings of the brain and spinal cord) are inflamed. Approximately 20% of amoxicillin binds to serum proteins in the blood, with therapeutic levels detected in interstitial (tissue) fluid after a standard dose.

Excretion and Metabolism

The body metabolizes and eliminates amoxicillin fairly quickly, with a half-life of about 61.3 minutes. Within six to eight hours of oral administration, roughly 60% of amoxicillin is excreted in the urine, primarily in its original form.

Probenecid, a medication sometimes used to treat gout, can slow amoxicillin excretion. If taken together, your doctor may adjust the amoxicillin dosage to maintain therapeutic levels.

Mechanisms of Bacterial Resistance

Resistance to amoxicillin occurs when bacteria develop mechanisms to neutralize the antibiotic's effectiveness. One common mechanism involves beta-lactamase enzymes, which break down the beta-lactam ring—a critical structural feature of amoxicillin. When this ring is broken, amoxicillin loses its ability to disrupt the bacterial cell wall.

> *Avoiding unnecessary use of antibiotics can reduce the chances of promoting antibiotic-resistant bacteria. This is why doctors prescribe antibiotics carefully, based on the infection's likely bacterial cause.*

Susceptibility Interpretive Criteria for Amoxicillin

Medical laboratories often test how effectively amoxicillin can combat specific bacterial strains, reporting results as susceptible, intermediate, or resistant:

- **Susceptible**: The antibiotic is expected to effectively inhibit the bacteria at usual concentrations in the body.
- **Intermediate**: Results are inconclusive; the antibiotic might work in specific settings, but re-testing or alternative treatments are suggested.
- **Resistant**: The bacteria are unlikely to respond to treatment with amoxicillin, and another antibiotic is needed.

Note: For infections caused by Helicobacter pylori, susceptibility tests for amoxicillin are not standardized. In cases where treatment fails, Clarithromycin susceptibility testing may be useful.

Quality Control in Susceptibility Testing

Laboratories use strict quality control standards to ensure the accuracy and reliability of susceptibility testing. These standards involve:

- Verifying that testing methods meet industry protocols
- Ensuring that amoxicillin's effectiveness falls within an expected **minimum inhibitory concentration (MIC)** range for common pathogens.

Suggestion: A table listing typical MIC ranges for various bacteria could help readers understand how amoxicillin's effectiveness is measured.

Quality Control Microorganism	Minimum Inhibitory Concentrations (mcg/mL)	Disc Diffusion Zone Diameter (mm)
Streptococcus pneumoniae ATCC[b] 49619	0.03 to 0.12	....
Klebsiella pneumoniae ATCC 700603	> 128	—

[a] QC limits for testing *E. coli* 35218 when tested on Haemophilus Test Medium (HTM) are ≥ 256 mcg/mL for amoxicillin; testing amoxicillin may help to determine if the isolate has maintained its ability to produce betalactamase[4].
[b] ATCC = American Type Culture Collection

Understanding how amoxicillin works helps patients appreciate the importance of following the prescribed dosage and duration. Proper use reduces the risk of bacterial resistance and ensures that amoxicillin can effectively target and eliminate infections.

Chapter 5: Pharmacological Interactions Between Amoxicillin and Other Drugs

When taking amoxicillin, it's important to be aware of potential interactions with other medications, which may either reduce its effectiveness or lead to increased side effects. Drug interactions can occur because of changes in how drugs are absorbed, distributed, metabolized, or excreted in the body.

Understanding Drug-Drug Interactions

What is a Drug Interaction?

A drug interaction happens when one medication alters the effect of another. This can lead to increased side effects or reduce a medication's effectiveness, making it important to discuss all current medications with your healthcare provider before starting amoxicillin.

- **Absorption**: Some drugs may increase or decrease how well amoxicillin is absorbed.
- **Distribution:** Compounds that displace amoxicillin from protein-binding sites may increase its level in the bloodstream.
- **Metabolism**: Certain drugs can either speed up or slow down how quickly amoxicillin is broken down by the body.
- **Excretion**: Medications that affect kidney function can change how quickly amoxicillin is excreted, potentially raising or lowering its concentration in the body.

Always inform your doctor of any prescription, over the counter, or herbal supplements you are taking to avoid possible interactions.

Common Drug Interactions with Amoxicillin

Below is a table summarizing some common drug interactions. For simplicity, here are key terms:

- **Increased Serum Level**: Leads to higher levels of amoxicillin in the bloodstream, potentially increasing side effects.

- **Reduced Serum Level**: Leads to lower levels of amoxicillin, possibly reducing its effectiveness.

Drug	Interaction with Amoxicillin
Aceclofenac	Reduces amoxicillin excretion, increasing serum levels
Acetaminophen	Slows amoxicillin excretion, increasing serum levels
Aspirin	Reduces amoxicillin excretion, potentially increasing side effects
Warfarin	May require additional blood tests as amoxicillin can increase its blood-thinning effect
Ibuprofen	Reduces amoxicillin excretion, increasing serum levels
Methotrexate	Can increase amoxicillin serum concentration, elevating risk of side effects
Allopurinol	Combined use may increase the risk of skin reactions with amoxicillin
Azithromycin	May reduce effectiveness of amoxicillin when used together
Oral Contraceptives	Amoxicillin may reduce effectiveness; consider additional contraception
BCG Vaccine	Amoxicillin may reduce vaccine effectiveness
Tetracyclines	Decrease effectiveness of amoxicillin when used concurrently

Probenecid	Reduces excretion of amoxicillin, increasing its serum levels
Rifampin	Can decrease amoxicillin levels, reducing its effectiveness
Vitamin K Antagonists	Increased risk of bleeding; may require monitoring of blood coagulation levels

If you're taking any of the above medications, consult your doctor to see if a dosage adjustment or additional monitoring is necessary.

Knowing the potential interactions between amoxicillin and other drugs can help you make informed decisions and reduce the risk of adverse effects. Always communicate with your healthcare provider about any medications or supplements you're using before starting amoxicillin.

Chapter 6: Dosage and Method of Application

It is essential to follow your doctor's instructions when taking amoxicillin to ensure effectiveness and prevent resistance. This chapter provides guidelines on dosing, application methods, and what to do if you miss a dose.

General Guidelines for Taking Amoxicillin

- **Follow the Prescription**: Only take amoxicillin as prescribed by your doctor, following the exact dose and timing.
- **With or Without Food**: Amoxicillin can be taken on an empty stomach or after eating without affecting its effectiveness.

For Liquid Medication Users:

- **Shake** Well: Shake the bottle thoroughly before each use to ensure the medication is evenly mixed.
- **Measure** Carefully: Use a medical measuring device to measure the exact dose. Avoid using household teaspoons, as they may not be accurate.
- **Mixing** with Beverages: You may mix the liquid with a small amount of cold beverages (milk, juice, or ginger ale), especially for children. Ensure that the child drinks the entire mixture promptly.

Even if you start feeling better, complete the full course of amoxicillin as prescribed. Stopping early may allow bacteria to survive and become resistant.

Dosage Guidelines

Amoxicillin dosage depends on the condition being treated, patient weight, and age. Always consult your doctor for exact dosing. Below are typical guidelines based on different scenarios:

General Dosage for Bacterial Infections:

Adults and Children Weighing Over 45 kg:

- **250-500 mg** three times a day, or
- **500-875 mg** twice a day, at the same intervals each day.

Children and Infants Weighing Less Than 40 kg:

- **Standard Dose**: 20-40 mg/kg of body weight every eight hours, or 25-45 mg/kg per day divided every 12 hours.
- **Infants Under Three Months**: The usual dose is 30 mg/kg per day, divided into two doses (every 12 hours).

For children, follow your pediatrician's specific recommendations based on weight and age.

Dosage for Specific Conditions

Gonorrhea Treatment:

For Adults, Adolescents, and Children Over 40 kg:
- Single Dose: 3 grams (g) of amoxicillin, typically combined with **Probenecid** at 25 mg/kg and **Methylprednisolone** at 50 mg/kg to enhance effectiveness.

Children Under 2 Years:
- Dosage determined by the doctor. Note: Amoxicillin is generally not recommended for children under two for gonorrhea.

H. pylori Infection:

Adults:
- **Dual Therapy**: 1000 mg of amoxicillin with 30 mg of lansoprazole every eight hours for 14 days.
- **Triple Therapy**: 1000 mg of amoxicillin, 500 mg of clarithromycin, and 30 mg of lansoprazole twice daily for 14 days.

Children:

- Dosage and duration are determined by the pediatrician.

Patient Category	Standard Dose	Notes
Adults & Children >45 Kg	250-500 mg three times daily or 500-875 mg twice daily	Exact dose and frequency as per doctor's instructions
Children Infants < 40 kg	20-40 mg/kg every 8 hours or 25-45 mg/kg/day divided every 12 hours	"Pediatrician determines exact dose; consult for specific cases
Infants < 3 Months	30 mg/kg/day divided into two doses (every 12 hours)	Consult pediatrician for exact dosage in young infants
Gonorrhea Treatment (Adults & Children > 40 Kg	Single dose of 3 g, combined with Probenecid and Methylprednisolone	Use additional drugs as specified by doctor
H. Pylori Infection (Adults)	Dual: 1000 mg Amoxicillin + 30 mg Lansoprazole every 8 hours for 14 days \triple: 1000 mg Amoxicillin + 500 mg Clarithromycin + 30 mg Lansoprazole twice daily for 14 days"	Alternative therapy based on doctor's assessment; pediatric dosage varies

If You Miss a Dose

- **Take It As Soon As Possible**: If you remember shortly after the missed dose, take it immediately.
- **Skip If Close to Next Dose**: If it's almost time for your next dose, skip the missed dose and return to your regular schedule.
- **Avoid Double Doses**: Never take two doses at once to make up for a missed dose.

Set a reminder on your phone or use a medication tracking app to help stay on schedule.

Adhering to the prescribed dosage and schedule for amoxicillin is essential for effective treatment. Consistency helps in fully eradicating infections and reducing the risk of antibiotic resistance.

Chapter 7: Side Effects

While amoxicillin is effective in treating bacterial infections, like any medication, it may cause some side effects. Most side effects are mild and manageable, but some may require medical attention. This chapter outlines common and serious side effects and provides guidance on when to consult a healthcare provider.

Common Side Effects of Amoxicillin

These mild side effects are relatively common and often resolve on their own. However, if they persist or cause discomfort, consult your doctor for advice on managing them.

- **Nausea**
- **Vomiting**
- **Diarrhea**
- **Stomachache**
- **Headache**

- **Rash** (often mild)
- **Swollen, black, or "hairy" tongue**
- **Cervical discomfort or leakage** (specific to some patients)

> *Taking amoxicillin with food can help reduce stomach-related side effects like nausea and stomachache.*

Serious Side Effects of Amoxicillin

Certain side effects are more severe and may indicate an allergic reaction or other serious conditions. If you experience any of the following, seek medical assistance immediately:

- **Clostridium difficile infection**: Overgrowth of Clostridium difficile bacteria in the intestines can cause colitis, a severe inflammation of the colon, leading to watery diarrhea, fever, and abdominal pain.
- **Fever and Chills**: Persistent fever may signal an adverse reaction.
- **Red or Watery Diarrhea**: Diarrhea accompanied by blood or persistent symptoms can be a sign of a severe infection.

- **Rash with Blisters or Peeling Skin**: Red or purple rashes with blistering or peeling can indicate a serious skin reaction.
- **Hives or Itching**: Swelling of the mouth or throat, itching, or difficulty breathing may suggest an allergic reaction.
- **Seizures**: Rare but possible; seek immediate medical attention.
- **Hepatitis**: Symptoms include yellowing of the skin (jaundice), fatigue, and abdominal pain.
- **Severe Stomach Cramps**

***Warning!** Allergic Reactions: Symptoms like hives, swelling of the mouth or throat, difficulty breathing, or an itchy rash can signal an allergic reaction. Seek emergency care if these occur.*

Managing Side Effects

For minor side effects, your doctor may suggest simple strategies or over-the-counter medications to reduce symptoms. Here are some general tips:

- **Diarrhea**: Avoid anti-diarrheal medications unless your doctor advises them, as these can sometimes worsen the condition.
- **Nausea or Stomach Pain**: Taking amoxicillin with food may help.
- **Headache:** Over-the-counter pain relievers (if approved by your doctor) may relieve headaches.

Drink plenty of fluids to stay hydrated, especially if experiencing diarrhea or vomiting.

While amoxicillin is generally safe, understanding potential side effects helps you recognize when to seek medical assistance. Always complete the full course of antibiotics, even if side effects occur, and consult your doctor about any symptoms that are severe or persistent.

Chapter 8: Pregnancy and Breastfeeding

Amoxicillin is generally safe to use during pregnancy and breastfeeding, but as with any medication, it's important to follow your doctor's guidance. This chapter explains the safety of amoxicillin for pregnant and breastfeeding mothers, potential side effects, and when to consult a healthcare provider.

Amoxicillin During Pregnancy

Amoxicillin, a penicillin-class antibiotic, is categorized as a Group B medication by the FDA, meaning it's generally considered safe for pregnant women. Animal studies have shown no harm to developing babies, and many medical experts approve its use during pregnancy if needed. However, always consult your doctor or gynecologist for the safest option, as each case is unique.

Other Safe Antibiotics During Pregnancy

Amoxicillin is not the only antibiotic that can be safely used during pregnancy. Other commonly prescribed antibiotics include:

- **Clindamycin**
- **Erythromycin**

Always ask your doctor to confirm the safest antibiotic choice if you need treatment during pregnancy.

How to Take Amoxicillin Safely During Pregnancy

If prescribed amoxicillin, follow the full treatment course to ensure the infection is completely resolved. Skipping doses or stopping early may lead to recurrence and increase the risk of antibiotic resistance.

Common Side Effects During Pregnancy

- **Diarrhea**
- **Nausea**
- **Vomiting**

If amoxicillin causes nausea, try taking it with food and a full glass of water to ease stomach discomfort.

Serious Side Effects to Watch For

While serious side effects are rare, it's important to be aware of symptoms that may require prompt medical attention, including:

- **Allergic Reactions**: Hives, swelling, or breathing difficulties.
- **Severe Diarrhea**: Persistent watery diarrhea or stomach cramps could indicate a secondary infection.
- **Yellowing of Skin or Eyes**: This may be a sign of liver issues.

Diarrhea lasting more than two days or occurring multiple times a day should be reported to your doctor. Severe diarrhea may require a different antibiotic to ensure the safety of both mother and baby.

Potential Risks and Benefits

Untreated bacterial infections during pregnancy can become serious and may pose risks to both mother and baby. Amoxicillin offers a low-risk option for treating infections safely at any pregnancy stage.

- **Risk of Infection**: Some infections, if left untreated, may lead to birth defects, respiratory issues, or growth complications for the baby.
- **Decision to Use Amoxicillin**: Your doctor will assess the type of infection and duration needed to treat it, balancing risks to provide safe and effective treatment.

Always check with your physician if you have any concerns about taking medications during pregnancy.

Pregnancy and Bacterial Infections

During pregnancy, the body naturally protects the baby from many common illnesses. However, some infections can still affect the baby, as the placenta does not block all pathogens. Certain infections can pose risks such as birth deformities, developmental issues, or respiratory problems.

- **Possible Complications**: Some untreated infections may increase the risk of miscarriage or other pregnancy complications.
- **When to Consult a doctor**: If you suspect an infection or have any symptoms, contact your physician promptly for advice.

Breastfeeding While Using Amoxicillin

Amoxicillin is generally safe for breastfeeding mothers. While small amounts of amoxicillin may pass into breast milk, it is unlikely to harm the baby. However, there are a few side effects to watch for:

- **Infant Diarrhea**: In rare cases, amoxicillin can cause diarrhea in breastfed infants.
- **Oral Thrush**: Overgrowth of natural flora in the baby's mouth may cause a condition called thrush.

If you notice diarrhea or signs of oral thrush in your baby, inform your doctor, who can provide guidance on how to manage these symptoms.

Amoxicillin is widely regarded as a safe antibiotic for pregnant and breastfeeding women. However, always consult with your healthcare provider to ensure it's the best choice for your specific condition and monitor for any side effects in yourself or your baby.

BONUS CHAPTER: FREQUENTLY ASKED QUESTIONS

1. Can I take amoxicillin on an empty stomach?

Yes, amoxicillin can be taken with or without food. However, if you experience stomach discomfort, nausea, or cramping, taking it with food can help minimize these effects.

2. Should I take a double dose of amoxicillin on the first day?

No, you should not take a double dose unless specifically instructed by your doctor. Follow your doctor's prescribed dose, typically divided into 2-3 doses daily, depending on your weight and condition.

3. What is the appropriate amoxicillin dosage for strep throat?

For strep throat, the CDC recommends:

- Children: 250 mg twice daily or 250 mg three times daily for 10 days.
- Adults and Adolescents: 250 mg four times daily or 500 mg twice daily for 10 days. Always follow your doctor's specific recommendations based on age, weight, and severity.

4. Can I drink alcohol while taking amoxicillin?

Yes, it is generally safe to drink alcohol in moderation while taking amoxicillin. However, avoiding alcohol may help your body focus on fighting the infection.

5. Can I take amoxicillin with paracetamol?

Yes, you can take amoxicillin and paracetamol together. This combination is safe, as long as you're not taking any conflicting medications. Follow all dosing instructions carefully.

6. What can be used as a substitute for amoxicillin?

For those who may have a sensitivity to amoxicillin, alternatives include:

- **Cefdinir (Omnicef), cefpodoxime (Cefzil)**, and **cefuroxime (Ceftin)**
- **Amoxicillin-clavulanate (Augmentin)** Consult your doctor for the best alternative based on your needs.

7. How is amoxicillin different from penicillin?

Amoxicillin covers a broader range of bacteria compared to penicillin, making it more effective for certain infections. Both belong to the penicillin class of antibiotics but differ in their bacterial targets.

8. What medications should not be taken with amoxicillin?

Avoid taking the following with amoxicillin unless advised by your doctor:

- **Antimicrobials** and **Live Typhoid Vaccine**
- **Penicillins and Methotrexate**
- **Penicillins and Select Anticoagulants (Vitamin K Antagonists)**
- **Oral Contraceptives** Always consult your healthcare provider to verify any potential interactions.

9. Is amoxicillin safe?

Amoxicillin is a widely used, safe, and cost-effective antibiotic. However, it's essential to only use it when prescribed for specific bacterial infections, as antibiotics are tailored to individual conditions.

10. What if I accidentally take a double dose of amoxicillin?

Taking an extra dose may not increase its effectiveness against bacteria but may cause side effects like diarrhea or stomach pain. Contact your healthcare provider if you're concerned or experience adverse symptoms.

11. Does amoxicillin treat acne?

Yes, research indicates amoxicillin can be helpful in treating inflammatory acne, particularly in cases where other treatments are ineffective. Consult a dermatologist for guidance on using antibiotics for acne.

12. Can amoxicillin cause heartburn?

Yes, some people may experience heartburn as a side effect, as antibiotics can sometimes irritate the stomach lining, increasing acid production. Consult your doctor if this becomes problematic.

13. Is it safe to take expired amoxicillin?

Taking expired amoxicillin is not recommended, as its effectiveness may decrease, potentially promoting antibiotic resistance. Always check expiration dates and properly dispose of expired medications.

14. Is a 3-day course of amoxicillin sufficient?

For some minor infections, a 3-day course may be adequate, but the standard treatment is typically 5-10 days. Follow your prescription duration exactly to ensure effective treatment.

15. Do I need to eat before taking amoxicillin?

No, you don't need to eat beforehand, but if you experience stomach discomfort, try taking amoxicillin with food. Swallow the pill whole with water—do not chew or crush it.

16. Why does amoxicillin cause diarrhea?

Diarrhea can occur as a side effect because antibiotics disrupt the balance of bacteria in the intestines. This change can allow harmful bacteria to flourish, causing stomach discomfort.

Printed by
Youcanprint

www.ingramcontent.com/pod-product-compliance
Lightning Source LLC
Chambersburg PA
CBHW071307030225
21338CB00015B/171